MAY 2004

RANDOLPH J. CALDECOTT

and the Story of the
Caldecott Medal

GREAT ACHIEVEMENT
A·W·A·R·D·S

P.O. Box 196
Hockessin, Delaware 19707

GREAT ACHIEVEMENT
A·W·A·R·D·S

Titles in the Series

Visit us on the web at www.mitchelllane.com
Comments? Email us at mitchelllane@mitchelllane.com

RANDOLPH J. CALDECOTT

and the Story of the Caldecott Medal

GREAT ACHIEVEMENT

A · W · A · R · D · S

Copyright © 2004 by Mitchell Lane Publishers, Inc. All rights reserved. No part of this book may be reproduced without written permission from the publisher. Printed and bound in the United States of America.

Printing   2   3   4   5   6   7   8   9

Library of Congress Cataloging-in-Publication Data

Bankston, John, 1974-
    Randolph J. Caldecott and the story of the Caldecott Medal / John Bankston.
       p. cm. — (Great achievement awards)
    Summary: A biography of the nineteenth-century English illustrator for children's books, for whom the Caldecott medal is named.
    Includes bibliographical references and index.
    ISBN 1-58415-200-1 (library)
     1. Caldecott, Randolph, 1846-1886—Juvenile literature. 2. Illustrators—England—Biography—Juvenile literature. 3. Illustrated children's books—Juvenile literature. 4. Illustration of books—Awards—United States—Juvenile literature. [1. Caldecott, Randolph, 1846-1886. 2. Illustrators. 3. Caldecott Medal.] I. Title. II. Series.
    NC978.5.C3B36 2003
    741.6'42'092—dc21
                                                2003004654

ABOUT THE AUTHOR: Born in Boston, Massachusetts, John Bankston has written over three dozen biographies for young adults profiling scientists like Jonas Salk and Alexander Fleming, celebrities like Mandy Moore and Alicia Keys, great achievers like Coretta Scott King, and master musicians like Franz Peter Schubert and Wolfgang Amadeus Mozart. An avid reader and writer, he has worked in Los Angeles, California as a producer, screenwriter and actor. Currently he is in pre-production on *Dancing at the Edge*, a semi-autobiographical film he hopes to film in Portland, Oregon. Last year he completed his first young adult novel, *18 to Look Younger*.

PHOTO CREDITS: Cover, p. 6: Aberdeen Art Gallery and Museum Collections; pp. 10, 16, 18, 19, 26, 29 Corbis; all other artwork, R. Caldecott.

PUBLISHER'S NOTE: The following story has been thoroughly researched and to the best of our knowledge represents a true story. Documentation of such research can be found on page 46.

    The Web sites referenced in this book were all active as of the publication date. Because of the fleeting nature of some internet sites, we cannot guarantee they will be active when you are reading this book.

TABLE OF CONTENTS

Attractive and healthy looking, Randolph Caldecott's charm opened doors long before his talent did. Sadly, he fought illnesses all his life, despite his appearance. His artwork, in many ways, was an escape from pain. This is a portrait he painted of himself in oils.

A FIERY START

The fire raged out of control. Flames leaped from broken windows as smoke poured into the cold night air, obscuring the stars. There was chaos everywhere as the Queen Railway Hotel was consumed by the blaze.

The hotel was located in Chester, England and conveniently sited across City Road from the railroad station. Not surprisingly, it was filled with travelers when the fire broke out.

Amid the destruction, patrons and employees streamed from open doors—coughing, their faces dark with soot. As they fled they passed into another crowd: the gathering hordes assembled around the blaze, enjoying it as they might enjoy a night at the theater. In the midst of the spectacle, a teenaged boy stood observing the inferno. He took in every detail.

He was tall for his age. His height made it easy for him to peer over the heads and shoulders of the other onlookers. He could see the center mezzanine, where many of the trapped victims wailed, and the top of the building where flames licked at the roof while the smokestacks were consumed. He watched as firefighters directed useless sprays of water into the third floor.

He recorded every detail.

In 1861, when the fire took place, cameras were cumbersome and difficult to use. Photographs required long exposure times. By the time the picture was taken, the scene was often over. Although photographers like Matthew Brady would take famous pictures during the Civil War, the best tool for capturing a detailed picture at that time was a good sketch pad, a drawing instrument and plenty of talent.

Young Randolph Caldecott was well prepared on all three counts.

The teenager was a high school dropout, working at a job he hated in the office of a bank. On that chilly night in December, the long years he'd spent idly drawing as a youngster paid off. His father believed that his son's talent was a useless hobby, but Randolph's drawing of that fire would be his first paying job.

Randolph Caldecott created children's pictures that had not been seen before. Here he shows a picture of a cat playing a violin.

The picture appeared in the *Illustrated London News* on December 7, 1861. It was the first time that he realized his gift for drawing could lead to a professional career instead of remaining a fantasy.

Success wouldn't come easy. He continued to work as a banker for another decade, often drawing sketches on receipts and envelopes as he struggled to earn a living from his art. He sold illustrations to newspapers and magazines, and studied nights at art schools. It was a struggle.

When Randolph finally achieved his greatest success, it wasn't as a newspaper artist. Instead he began drawing illustrations for children's books. During the nineteenth century, literacy had escalated. As more and more people began to read, more books were sold. Parents were reading to their children and the demand for short, highly readable texts grew. In many of these books, the pictures were just as important as the story.

Although children's books had been around for over 100 years, by the time Randolph illustrated them publishers were demanding high quality works. Randolph met their demands with illustrations that did more than just match the words. Every drawing he created added something to the text. Sometimes he added sadness, sometimes he added humor. Even the simplest and most familiar nursery rhymes seemed brand new whenever Randolph drew the pictures. His work was praised by critics and celebrated by the public.

In his illustrations accompanying "Hey Diddle Diddle," when the "Dish ran away with the Spoon," the dish is caught by the spoon's parents, Mr. Knife and Mrs. Fork. They drag the spoon away, while the dish is shattered into pieces, overseen by other weeping plates and saucers.

As an illustrator Randolph created action pictures unlike any that had been seen before. The characters he drew ran across the page, they leaped and did somersaults.

But in real life, Randolph couldn't do many of the things that these active, healthy characters did so easily. Even in his drawings for children, he often referred to his poor health. In the book *The Babes in the Wood*, he used himself as a model for the "gentleman of good account, sore sick and like to die."

Randolph indeed had a brief life. Although he died at a relatively young age, he still serves today as an inspiration to many illustrators the world over.

For that reason Randolph Caldecott had an award named after him by the American Library Association. Every year, the ALA recognizes the very best in children's book illustrations. The winner receives the Caldecott Medal.

Horses and buggies compete for road space in this scene from late 19th century London. The city provided Randolph with both amusement and inspiration.

CHAPTER 2

BANKING ON A DREAM

A traveler to the town of Chester in the 1840s would have noticed an area along Bridge Street nicknamed "The Row." Rising several feet above street level, a covered walkway ran alongside the doors of the street's businesses. Staircases jutted out here and there; beneath their planks children played games of hide-and-go-seek. It was a vibrant, exciting neighborhood, and few of the business people in the area were as respected or as successful as John Caldecott.

Caldecott had been trained as an accountant, and that education provided him with a talent for making the most of his money. However, he didn't work in the profession he was trained for. Instead he earned a living as a tailor and clothing store owner where he designed custom-made hats and suits. He was a hard worker and made a good living. Because he'd eventually father 13 children, he needed all the money he could get.

Like most of the neighboring shopkeepers, Caldecott maintained a small apartment for his family over his business. The space felt crowded with just his wife Mary Dinah and two small sons (though the second boy died just before the age of two). The space grew even more cramped with the arrival of the Caldecotts' third son, Randolph, who was born on March 22, 1846.

Two years after Randolph's birth, the family moved to a larger space, the Challoner House on Bridge Street. Not long afterward, Randolph contracted rheumatic fever. The disease was very common in children when he was growing up. It was also highly contagious. Children who got rheumatic fever were usually confined to their rooms and isolated from just about everyone. It was probably a lonely time for the future illustrator.

The disease would leave Randolph's heart permanently weakened. For the rest of his life he would tire easily and be underweight and pale. His younger brother Alfred referred to him as "always delicate."

Despite the price rheumatic fever extracted, the illness may also have changed Randolph in a more positive way. He probably discovered his talent while he was lying in bed suffering from inflamed joints and dizzy with fever.

Being sick as a child is something Randolph had in common with many artists and writers of his era. Forced to lie in bed for weeks at a time, these future creators didn't have much to do. They didn't have TV or video games to keep them entertained, and reading books wasn't always comfortable. All they had was their imaginations.

Randolph's body was confined to bed but his mind could go anywhere. He may have begun drawing on those long sick days, sketching the outdoors from memory or drawing the world outside his room where rheumatic fever imprisoned him.

When he was well, he went for long walks in the countryside. He was especially interested in the animals he saw. From the age of six, he was carving animals out of wooden blocks, modeling them in clay and drawing them.

But he'd scarcely recovered when he was forced to endure more hardship. In August of 1852, his mother Mary Dinah died. Some stories claim she was the supportive parent, the one who encouraged her son's dreams, the one who would have admired his first artistic efforts. Losing a parent as a child is tough for anyone, but Randolph probably also lost his protector. His father grew even more strict.

John Caldecott didn't stay a widower for long. He married another woman about two years later, and continued to have children. In short order Randolph had to cope with the loss of his mother, his father's remarriage and six new half brothers and half sisters.

Attending school helped take Randolph's mind off his troubles. His drawing did the rest. He enrolled at The Kings School, which had been founded by King Henry VllI in 1541. Despite an excellent reputation, the school wasn't exactly crowded. During the time Randolph attended, there were fewer than two dozen other students.

As a result, it wasn't easy to "blend into the woodwork," although Randolph may have tried. He was a scrawny kid, slight for his age because of his illness. Although he'd eventually grow to be taller than most other men, Randolph was one of the smaller boys when he began school, even among those his own age. He could often be seen hunched over a desk, his curly hair hanging in front of his eyes as he sketched pictures or built clay models. A watercolor painting he made of the church refectory was kept long after he left, and admired long before he was famous.

It remains there today.

Still, according to Arthur Locker, the editor of the *Graphic* magazine, most of Randolph's early work didn't stand out as much. Quoted in Rodney Engen's book *Randolph Caldecott: Lord of the Nursery*, Locker told of buying an old school book of Randolph's he found at a bookstall. Almost every inch of blank space in the margins was "adorned with sundry pen and ink sketches, exhibiting, however it must be frankly said, no more special talent than is shown by scores of lads who have a turn for drawing. It was only gradually that Caldecott discovered his real vocation."

Randolph was far from a natural talent. He had to work at drawing in order to get good at it. His strongest gift seemed to be the ability to take inspiration wherever he could find it, and his time at school inspired him for the rest of his life. Many of his later illustrations used the church's refectory and other school locations as models. Randolph did well at The Kings School, rising to head boy, an honor given both for academic achievement and for earning the respect of his peers. Despite his success and the opportunity to take classes at the nearby Cheshire School of Art, Randolph wasn't that involved with school by the time he reached his mid-teens.

When his father moved the family in 1860 to a larger home in Boughton, Randolph lost interest in school altogether. The next year he dropped out.

His father was not happy.

John Caldecott refused to let his offspring waste time on a ridiculous fantasy. If his son wanted to abandon his education, then he would work.

Using his connections, Randolph's father arranged for Randolph to get a job at the Whitchurch branch of Whitchurch Ellesmere Bank. Whitchurch was about 20 miles from Chester, far enough away from home that Randolph had to move out. Considering the tension that must have existed between him and his father, the decision was for the best.

Only 15 years old, Randolph had to find a place to live and take care of himself for the first time. He rented a room in a farmhouse two miles outside of town and began his job as a bank clerk.

He hated it. Because he hated it, he also wasn't very good at it.

It wasn't a matter of attitude. Randolph owned such a positive personality that he was easily recalled by co-workers years after he left the job. One of his fellow bank clerks vividly recalled Randolph and told the *Manchester Guardian* newspaper many years later, "We who knew him can well understand how welcome he must have been in many a cottage, farm and hall. The handsome lad carried his own recommendation. With light brown hair falling with a ripple over his brow, blue-gray eyes shaded by long lashes, sweet and mobile mouth, tall and well-made, he joined to these physical advantages a good humor and a charming disposition. No wonder that he was a general favorite."

It's a good thing he was so popular. Randolph failed miserably selling insurance, a significant part of every bank clerk's income in the 1860s. Going door to door selling for his bank, he didn't have a problem getting *into* the cottages. The challenge was making a sale by the time he left.

A friend of Randolph's named James Estes told a story that appears in Elizabeth Billington's book *The Randolph Caldecott Treasury.* According to Estes, after numerous failures Randolph finally convinced a farmer to take out a life insurance policy. When the time arrived for the farmer to come to the bank to sign the paperwork and pay for the insurance, he said to Randolph, "Now look 'ere, Mr. Caldecott, let us understand each other. If I pay this money, and am alive and well this day twelve month (one year later), your company will pay me 500 pounds."

Estes remembered Randolph being nearly speechless as he sputtered, "Oh, dear, no! If you die before the time your representatives will receive 500 pounds."

"That is not good enough for me," the farmer reportedly replied, taking his money and his business out the door.

Most of Randolph's experiences ran along the same lines. At least his hopeless sales calls left him with plenty of time to sketch the gorgeous countryside outside Whitchurch. It may have been one of the most miserable times of his life, but through it all he created art. Strolling along Down High Street where the bank was located or riding a horse to the farmhouses, Randolph was rarely without a sketch pad. Drawings he made of the parish church, the balconies overhanging the streets near his bank and the large tower of nearby St. Oswald's Church in Malpas would appear years later in his published illustrations. So would images of fishing and shooting, markets and cattle fairs.

Past the 200-year-old gates of St. Oswald's, during morbid or sad times, he could enter the cemetery and see the graves of Caldecotts who'd come before him. Touring the smooth gravestones of long-dead relatives, Randolph couldn't ignore his own declining health.

Despite his struggles, Randolph's dashing good looks and vibrant personality assured him a never-ending supply of friends and female companions. Letters he wrote from the time provided details of all the parties and dances he attended and the women he dated. Most of his letters included a personal touch, a tiny illustration decorating the address and date at the top of the page. The habit continued throughout his life.

Less than a year after his arrival in Whitchurch, he sold his first drawing. It was the illustration depicting the Queen's Railway Hotel fire. The sale helped Randolph believe he could someday be a professional artist. Others noticed the skill in the work, which he did despite the distractions of the crowds, the fire fighters and the blaze itself. Based on the drawing, Randolph began to get other assignments from magazines and newspapers.

Shortly before the age of 21, Randolph met William Langton, a managing director for the Manchester and Salford Bank. Randolph asked for a job. He got it.

Although unsuccessful in his career as a banker, Randolph's time in Whitchurch allowed him to draw detailed sketches of the countryside and various landmarks, including several well-known pictures of the St. Oswald's Church in nearby Malpas. This is a recent photograph of St. Oswald's Church.

CHAPTER 3

CITY LIGHTS

M anchester was one of the richest cities in all of England. Filled with energy and nightlife that had been completely lacking in sleepy Whitchurch, Randolph Caldecott could have been overwhelmed by such a dramatic change. Instead he took it in stride, pulling in as much from the vibrant urban environment as he could and putting it in his drawings. The city boasted the oldest library in England and a dozen daily newspapers, all of which would help the young artist. Still, nothing fed his artistic passion like Manchester itself.

"Caldecott used to wander about the bustling, murky streets of Manchester, sometimes finding himself in queer out-of-the-way quarters often coming across an odd character, curious bits of antiquity and the like," recalled old friend William Clough as quoted in Engen's book. "Whenever the chance came he made short excursions into the adjacent country, and long walks which were never purposeless. Whilst in this city so close was his application to the art that he loved that on several occasions he spent the whole night drawing."

The long hours of drawing made for some tired days at the bank, but to Randolph it was worth it. He'd sold illustrations to newspapers and magazines while in Whitchurch, but the move to Manchester brought him a renewed focus. Since he hadn't been involved in any type of formal training since dropping out of high school, he enrolled at the Manchester School of Art as an evening student.

Though Randolph didn't stay long at the school, his time there sharpened his line technique and improved his craft. Still, he never got as much from the school professionally as he did from his social life.

He joined the Brasenose Club, an exclusive social club for gentlemen with backgrounds in the arts and sciences. Surrounded by so many successful peers, Randolph's motivation only increased.

Founded two years after his arrival in Manchester, the club quickly grew to be a center of the city's cultural life. Because its founders were among the elite of Manchester's artistic community, Randolph quickly gained the contacts he needed to advance in his profession. Soon he was selling illustrations to a variety of magazines and newspapers.

He became a sort of freelance reporter, doing sketches of newsworthy events for a number of publications while also participating in the production of several short-lived magazines. He even got to have his work exhibited, showing a hunting illustration he called "At the Wrong End of the Wood" in 1869 at the Royal Manchester Institution.

Despite all of his success as an artist, Randolph found his working life to be just as tedious as it had been in Whitchurch. "There was seldom

visible in me any sober respect for the work of the bank," he confessed in a letter to William Clough that is quoted in Engen's book. To kill time he played an occasional practical joke and secretly sketched customers as they entered.

Yet for all of its charms, Manchester was not the best location for an aspiring artist. In nineteenth century England, that city was London, a place where artists such as George du Maurier and the American James Whistler lived and worked.

Mark Lemon (the editor of Punch magazine) would prove to be an early fan of Randolph's work.

In May of 1870, Randolph traveled to London, a portfolio of his drawings tucked beneath his arm. His Brasenose contacts helped him arrange a meeting with a successful older artist named Thomas Armstrong, who was immediately struck by Randolph's talent. For the rest of the illustrator's life, Armstrong would be his friend and mentor. Between Armstrong and his Brasenose friends, Randolph's sales slowly increased.

Armstrong introduced him to Mark Lemon, editor of *Punch* Magazine. The humor publication would later use a number of Randolph's drawings, but his first experience there was not so positive. Although he submitted a sketch and a book of drawings, the sketch never appeared and the book was lost.

The setback didn't discourage him. After returning to Manchester, he continually mailed sketches and drawings to London. Several of his illustrations did appear in 1871 in a publication called *London Society,*

Successful artists such as George du Maurier (left) and James Whistler (right) called London home.

whose editor Henry Blackburn would soon have a profound influence on Randolph's life.

Early in 1872, Randolph sold two paintings. Coupled with encouragement and advice from his friends, those sales gave the young artist the courage to take a major gamble. He quit his job at the bank and took his sketchpad and his dreams to London. He was abandoning a steady job with a secure income. Now his income would be determined by his ability to produce drawings and make sales.

As he recalled in an interview with the *Pall Mall Gazette* that is included in *Randolph Caldecott: Lord of the Nursery*, "I had the money in my pocket sufficient to keep me for a year or so, and was hopeful that during that time my powers would be developed and my style improved so much that I should find plenty of work."

But there were no guarantees. If he failed it would be back to banking—or worse.

When he reached London, he moved into an apartment building across from the British Museum on 46 Great Russell Street where he lived and worked on the upper floors. The open studio space provided excellent lighting for his work (at least when London wasn't overcast) but climbing the steep and twisting flights of stairs to get there couldn't have been easy for him.

Randolph also continued his formal arts education. Armstrong introduced him to a prominent artist, Sir Edward Poynter. Although the young illustrator hadn't attended the Manchester School of Art for some time, being in the new city motivated him to begin attending life drawing classes. The course where he learned how to accurately draw models was taught by Poynter; the painter had only recently begun the program at the Slade School of University College.

When Randolph wasn't busy with his career or his studies, he expanded his professional contacts. Many of the artists he'd admired from afar such as Whistler and du Maurier (a regular *Punch* contributor) became close friends. Like them, Randolph found an important new source of income—professional commissions. Commissions came when an artist was hired, usually by a wealthy patron, to produce a specific work of art such as a portrait. One of Randolph's best known commissions was a series of decorative panels adorned with very detailed birds which he rendered in oil for Henry Renshaw's home.

Yet in the midst of all these wonderful changes, a cloud as gray as any in London hung over Randolph's. He was getting weaker. Though he was an attractive young man, tall and athletic looking, his close friends saw how sick he seemed to be. The rheumatic fever which ripped into his childhood now tore into his adult life. London's damp and chilly climate contributed to his problems. He also wasn't cut out for the stresses of newspaper reporting— traveling around the city, getting stories and meeting deadlines. Between the long hours of reporting, his studies and his social activities, Randolph was overwhelmed. His health deteriorated.

But these difficulties couldn't take away his sense of humor. One letter to the editor of Blackburn's *London Society* asserted that Randolph was unable to draw women. His response was a sketch in which he drew himself holding up a cup with the word "inspiration" on it while working on a portrait of a seated female model.

In late 1872, Blackburn suggested that Randolph contribute some illustrations to a travel book he was working on. Though Blackburn had a reputation as a hard driving editor who was usually a difficult boss, he seemed to have a special place in his heart for Randolph. He invited Randolph to join him and his wife for several weeks during the summer while they toured the Harz Mountains in central Germany.

The book that resulted was called *The Harz Mountains: A Tour in the Toy Country.* Randolph contributed two dozen illustrations. It was the first book Randolph illustrated. It was well-received, but few of the work's readers could possibly know the depths of Randolph's talent.

They were about to find out.

Cover illustration for The Harz Mountains: A Tour in the Toy Country, 1873. This was the first book to contain Randolph's illustrations.

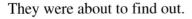

Edmund Evans was one of the most respected engravers in the world when he hired Randolph. Here is a portrait of the young artist, engraved and printed by Evans.

CHAPTER 1

THE OLD WOODPECKER

No matter how talented an illustrator was, his efforts were at the mercy of an engraver. Engravers were craftspeople, just like illustrators. But they owned a skill which like blacksmithing is almost obsolete today.

Just as good editors can improve a writer's work, sharp engravers could refine the pictures an illustrator created. In the nineteenth century, there wasn't any high-tech equipment. Each drawing an illustrator made had to be carved onto blocks of wood which were inked and placed in printing presses.

It was up to the engraver to find the talent. They would take on a writer's work, then hire illustrators to make the pictures that would accompany the text. After the project was complete, they'd sell it to a publisher. Then they'd take their engravings to a printing press.

One of those engravers was about to give Randolph a job.

Randolph's work on *The Harz Mountains* led to higher paying jobs including sales to several New York publications, including *Harper's New Monthly Magazine* and *New York Daily Graphic*. Still, by the end of 1873 he realized illustrating books rather than magazines would provide him with both longer terms of employment and better pay.

Most creative types are terrible business people. Very few artists have a "head for figures." Here Randolph was unique. His time as a banker made him much more sensible in financial affairs than his artistic peers. This skill would serve him well for the rest of his career.

When top British engraver James Cooper paid Randolph a visit in January of 1874, he was ready.

Cooper was already acquainted with Randolph's talent. He'd engraved one of the artist's illustrations, "A Debating Society," for *London Society* Magazine. There was no question that Randolph had the talent for the project Cooper had in mind. The question was whether or not he had the work ethic.

Washington Irving was a famous American writer whose greatest claim to fame was probably *The Legend of Sleepy Hollow,* the story of the hapless school teacher Ichabod Crane and his encounter with the "headless horseman." The project Cooper pitched that cold winter's day was nothing quite so dark. It was a holiday story called *Old Christmas: Selections from the Sketchbook* that Irving had written. This series of stories would require more than 100 illustrations. Though Irving had been dead for well over a decade, he was still a very popular author.

Cooper brought a copy of the text over to Randolph's Russell Street apartment. Cooper called himself "the old woodpecker." Considering the project he was taking on, the name was apt. After all, if Randolph agreed, Cooper would need to "peck" every mark the young artist made into blocks of wood. So when Cooper met with Randolph he made sure the artist knew exactly what was involved.

Randolph took his time in deciding. Transforming the words of a popular author into an illustrated book was as challenging then as making a movie from a beloved novel is today. As he carefully read the book, Irving's words created pictures in his mind, pictures he knew he could draw. *Pictures he must draw.*

"Went all through it," Randolph wrote in his diary. "I like the idea."

Eagerly he told Cooper he'd take the job. Randolph was drawing before the month was out. For nearly all of 1874, he labored on just that one project. By the time it was completed he'd created 120 illustrations. Most were extraordinarily detailed. His pictures showed the rich in top hats and tails, children with their chubby cheeks and winter scenes where the reader could almost *feel* the cold.

He also showed an affection for dogs, as canines of nearly every shape, size and breed filled the pages. The work was an effective lead-in to one of his future assignments, an article entitled "The Character of

Dogs." Published in February of 1884, the piece was unique not just for the incredibly detailed drawings but also for the piece's author: Robert Louis Stevenson, the author of *Treasure Island*.

When Randolph finished with the drawings for *Old Christmas*, he had a long wait. Each picture he drew had to be engraved and the process took Cooper nearly a year.

Randolph's patience was rewarded in October of 1875 when Macmillan and Company published *Old Christmas from the Sketch Book of Washington Irving, Illustrated by Randolph Caldecott*. It was an immediate success. The book not only sold well, it was also highly praised by critics who singled out Randolph's illustrations. There were so many positive reviews that a typically humble Randolph drew a sketch of himself growing tired as Cooper read one after another.

Randolph didn't spend much time soaking up the praise and basking in his new success. Instead he immediately began working on another Washington Irving book. Rarely taking time off between projects was a pattern Randolph had begun developing as soon as he moved to London. Despite his recent success, he knew he couldn't afford to rest.

In fact he and Cooper worked twice as hard; despite doing nearly as many drawings the project was completed in half the time. Irving's *Bracebridge Hall: Selections from the Sketch Book* was published in 1877.

Although well reviewed, it never sold as well as *Old Christmas*. Still, it caught the eye of another talented engraver. While Cooper gave Randolph professional opportunities, Edmund Evans would change the artist's life.

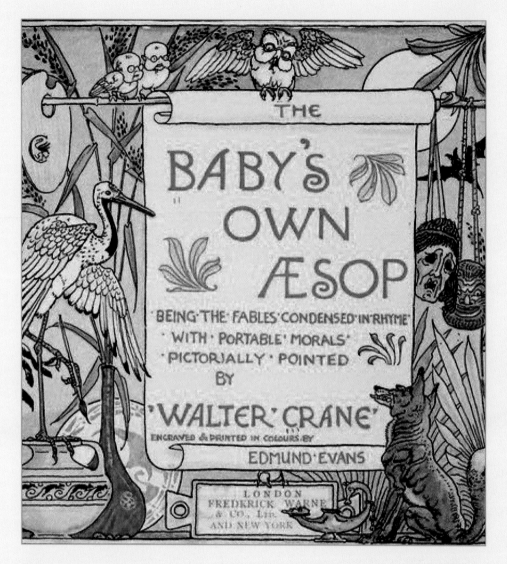

THE BABY'S OWN ÆSOP
BEING·THE·FABLES·CONDENSED·IN·RHYME·
·WITH·PORTABLE·MORALS·
·PICTORIALLY·POINTED·
BY
'WALTER·CRANE'
ENGRAVED & PRINTED IN COLOURS BY
EDMUND·EVANS

LONDON
FREDRICK WARNE
& CO., Ltd.
AND NEW YORK

Today, movie producers put together all the elements needed to make a movie; in the 1800s, engravers put together all the elements needed to make a book, including the writers, the artists, and the printers. They often had a credit on the cover, as Edmund Evans does in this book by Walter Crane.

A New Career

E dmund Evans was head and shoulders above other engravers. For one thing, he had moved from black and white to color pictures. Crafting a book with colored drawings required using several wood blocks for each picture. Each block held a different color. When pressed into a single page, they combined for the final result.

Besides his talent for color engraving, Evans was also a sharp businessman. He'd taken advantage of a trend which had begun more than a century earlier to become successful.

The year 1744 marked a revolution in literature. That was the year that John Newbery embarked on a new career. A London magazine publisher and medicine maker, Newbery turned to book publishing. He quickly recognized an enormous untapped market: children.

Up to that point, children had been almost entirely ignored in publishing. The few books written for them were educational. There were almost no stories published for their entertainment. John Newbery changed all of that.

At his business on 65 Saint Paul's Churchyard, he added a sign that read "Juvenile Library." It complemented his window decorations of the sun and a Bible. Then he began to publish.

Newbery would eventually produce over 200 textbooks and books for adults. But it is the books he published for children that are still remembered today, more than 250 years later. Newbery's *A Little Pretty Pocket Book* was the first book exclusively for children and their entertainment.

Kids whose only other books were school texts eagerly sought out these new books. Before he died, Newbery published nearly two dozen books for children. His success encouraged others to follow his lead.

Charles Welsh writes in *A Bookseller of the Last Century* that "Newbery was not an educator. He was a benevolent book seller. He saw that children's books could be important in his business, and he developed them with taste and enthusiasm. They proved by their success that they met a need."

After Newbery's death, this need was met by a variety of publishers. By the 1870s, the reading public was generally better educated and more affluent. They weren't interested in the cheap, disposable looking books which had been popular a generation before.

It was an amazing time for Randolph to be alive. His talent as an illustrator was matched by the quality of books being published.

Publishers were utilizing improving technologies to create books which were as great to look at as they were to read. Evans was one of these publishers. His books for children were attractively bound and covered on thick paper. However, he quickly realized it wasn't just the look of the book that counted, it was what was inside it. He hired the best writers and illustrators, including artists Kate Greenaway and Walter Crane.

Randolph and Crane were already close friends. They had been introduced to each other by the artist Thomas Armstrong. In the beginning, Randolph was slightly awed by the more successful Crane. Although the two were close in age, Crane was better known. He was not, however, entirely successful financially. In those days, most illustrators were paid by the job—it didn't matter if their books sold one copy or one million. To Randolph that policy seemed unfair. After all, weren't the illustrations a major factor in a book's success? Shouldn't the artist share part of that success?

Randolph got his chance to test this idea in early 1878. Crane left Evans and the engraver desperately needed another illustrator. Reading through the two Irving books that Randolph had illustrated, Evans was stunned by the artist's craft. He arranged a meeting. Again Randolph was ready.

Evans explained what he hoped to do—create a series of high quality picture books for children which Randolph would illustrate. It was an ideal situation for Randolph. He was free to choose the subjects.

While the engraver had paid Crane by the job, he agreed to a different arrangement with Randolph. A small percentage of the cover price, called a royalty, was included in the deal. Randolph would get six and a half percent. It was a start.

As time-consuming as Randolph's work had been before, this project was even more labor-intensive. The pictures—outlines really—went to the engraver, who carved out blocks of wood. These were then turned into colored engravings. Evans used six colors for one of Randolph's books— red, blue, yellow, pink, brown, and gray.

Children's illustrator Walter Crane was far better known than Randolph, although they were the same age. Still, Randolph's banking experience made him sharper with money and soon, he was earning more than Crane.

Randolph was almost certainly a bit nervous as the publication date drew nearer late in 1878. These were the first books he'd done for children. Would the talent he had shown in his drawing for adults translate to a younger audience?

He didn't have to wait long. Once again a book Randolph helped create arrived just in time for Christmas (even in the nineteenth century, people thought books made great presents). Thirty thousand copies each of *John Gilpin* and *The House That Jack Built* went on sale in December. Within six months they would all be sold. While Randolph would complain in a letter to Walter Clough that "I get a small royalty —a small, small royalty," he'd earn nearly 400 pounds. That was four times what he'd earned in his last year as a bank clerk.

His books did more than sell well; they were described in glowing terms by nearly every reviewer. "His *John Gilpin* and *The House That Jack Built* are sui generis [unique] and irresistibly funny as well as clever," said one piece in *The Nation*. "Happy [is] the generation that is brought up on such masters as Mr. Caldecott and Mr. Walter Crane."

Previously, Randolph had grown tired while he listened to Cooper read the reviews of his books. This time was different. He was invested in the books, and he knew good reviews would only help sales. The more he sold, the more money he made.

Being compared to Crane must have been a heady experience for the illustrator. Still he knew he wanted to do better monetarily than Crane. Although relationships between artists and their employers are often adversarial — filled with disagreements over money and creative control—Randolph and Evans became close friends during the time they collaborated on the first two books. Some engravers tried to influence the artists they hired. Evans didn't.

By allowing his illustrators to enjoy creative freedom, he gained their trust; by faithfully reproducing their work, he earned their respect. Despite trusting and respecting the engraver, Randolph realized how important he was to Evans. After all, the first printing sold out. So Randolph asked for a raise. Evans was reluctant, because increasing Randolph's percentage might mean raising the price of the books. That could hurt sales. Evans asked Randolph to be patient.

Randolph was already beginning the next two books, *Elegy on the Death of a Mad Dog* and *The Babes in the Wood*. *The Babes in the Wood* was far darker than the first two and earned mixed reviews when it came out in December of 1879 for its humorous treatment of death. Since Randolph himself had an intimate relationship with his own mortality, the criticism may have been unfounded. Besides, if positive reviews of his first book helped him make a case to Evans for more money, in a way negative reviews of his second only improved his case. For by now, Randolph seemed to be "review proof." The parents who bought the books for their kids were responding to their children's requests, so they no longer cared about reviews. Children were asking for Randolph's books by name.

It still took two years before Randolph got his raise—to 10 percent. Eventually he earned 12 1/2 percent of the cover price.

Above: Cover of The House That Jack Built

In the 1870s, Randolph's books sold so well that he earned many times what he would have as a bank clerk. In some cases, he even re-wrote popular stories in addition to illustrating them.

Below: Cover of John Gilpin

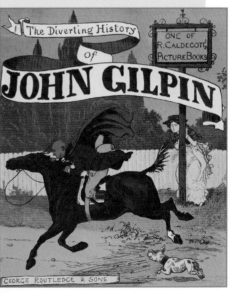

In this illustration from John Gilpin, *Randolph demonstrates his love for dogs, fast horses, and his attention to detail (notice the expressions on the children on the balcony.)*

In all, he would produce 16 "Picture Books" for Evans. Describing himself in an interview with the *Pall Mall Gazette* that is included in Engen's book, Randolph explained, "When Mr. Caldecott is contemplating one of his children's picture-books he chooses his own subjects, and after a good deal of serious consideration as to the method of treatment to be applied, he makes a blank book of the required size and rapidly draws a number of sketches in the rough page for page as they will appear." He only did this once. Randolph rarely revised his work. It's little wonder, considering how tight his deadlines were.

Sometimes he used existing works, either stories or rhymes, to illustrate. Often he would add more words. A few times he even wrote the books, which must have added quite a bit to his workload.

Estimates of the total sales of the books vary widely. Randolph's relatives had every reason to say he sold more, Evans had every reason to say he sold less. By some calculations, well over 800,000 copies were sold during Randolph's lifetime, providing him with an income that made him rich by the standards of nineteenth century England.

Rich and single.

With the success of the first books insuring him of a stable income, the artist sought a stable life.

Randolph was 33 when *John Gilpin* and *The House That Jack Built* were published. Although he'd had numerous girlfriends, he'd never settled down. While this is common today, it was out of the ordinary in an era when many people married as teenagers. Randolph realized he was ready for a different life. And maybe, just maybe, a wife.

To some, death was not an appropriate subject for children, and Randolph's The Babes in the Wood, *got poor reviews because of this. Yet, the dark theme and lavish illustrations gave him a larger audience. His audience grew even larger when he added new illustrations to later editions.*

No matter how much time he spent in the cities, Randolph never lost his love for the country. His dreams of ideal country life are obvious in this illustration, "The Farmer's Boy," from The Picture Book *(1881).*

CHAPTER 6

A QUIET LIFE

By 1879 Randolph Caldecott was successful but his work load was wearing him down. As much as he loved bustling London, the city wasn't exactly helping his health. It had been over a decade since he'd lived in a rural area, and now he decided to return to country life. In the fall he bought a small house called Wybournes, at Kemsing in Kent County.

The decision to relocate did more than improve his health. It also introduced him to the woman who would be with him for the rest of his life.

Marian Brind lived with her family in a house beside the Church of St.-Martin-of-Tours, seven miles from Randolph's home. He didn't waste much time. Although there is little information about where and when the couple met, they seemed to begin courting almost as soon as the artist's arrival in Wybournes. This form of organized dating, which usually led to marriage, meant Randolph regularly made the 14-mile roundtrip journey on horseback along Childsbridge Way to Marian's house in Chelsfield.

The couple were married on March 18, 1880. Randolph's younger brother was now a minister and presided over the ceremony, which was held at St. Martin's Church, Marian and her attendants walked to the wedding from her house.

Having been a bachelor for so long, Randolph's life was immediately changed by the marriage. "Breakfast at eight—and no nonsense. Work from nine to two," he wrote his friends.

Marriage added to his stability as Randolph added to his workload. Besides his regular schedule of two books every year for Evans, he also illustrated three books for the noted children's book writer Juliana Horatia Ewing in the early 1880s: *Daddy Darwin's Dovecote*, *Lob Lie-by-the-Fire* and *Jackanapes*.

"I have a large quantity of work promised to be done between now and August," he complained in a letter to Ewing, "and I have had to give up [for] the present carrying out some drawings, which have been expected any time during the last few months."

In the fall of 1882, Randolph again heard London calling. The couple took a long-term lease on a house in London. But he may not have been happy. In a doodle adorning a letter to a friend, drawn during Christmas of 1882, a dead bird lies in the doorway while "Not at home" is scrawled alongside the elegant cursive address. The couple had gone to stay with Marian's relatives.

Traveling away from his house was habit. Always a traveler from the time of his first success, Randolph had sometimes spent winters in such warm and exotic locales as the French Riviera and the Italian coast. In the winter of 1885, a poet friend named Frederick Locker suggested that Randolph and Marian should tour North America. It would be part business, part pleasure. Randolph would sketch scenes of the United States as he and his wife made their way south from New York to Florida. The warm weather in the south would be good for Randolph's declining health, Locker believed.

He was wrong.

For Randolph, who was always in fragile health, the problems began immediately. While trans-Atlantic travel was common by the late nineteenth century, it was never very pleasant. The ocean crossing was rough. Cramped and noisy

Caldecott illustrated books for a number of successful children's authors, including Juliana Horatio Ewing. This is his cover for Daddy Darwin's Dovecoat.

quarters were standard as much of the space on the ship was taken up by the equipment needed to run it. The North Atlantic route from England to New York was particularly treacherous (it would claim the *Titanic* nearly three decades later) but by all accounts the artist stayed in good spirits. He did jokingly cable his friends at home that he hoped an "overland route" would be ready by the time he made the return trip.

There was, of course, no "overland route." It wouldn't have made any difference. Randolph never made the return trip.

Designed to expose Randolph to every aspect of the nineteenth century United States, including California, the trek would have been ambitious even a century later. Still, letters from Randolph were upbeat as he sketched the cities he saw: New York, Philadelphia, Washington, D.C. But shortly after he drew what would be his last sketch in Charleston, his condition grew rapidly worse.

Randolph and Marian arrived in northern Florida in mid-December as the state suffered through a brutal cold spell, the worst it had experienced in 50 years. The unusual weather would last through the new year. Between the chilly climate and the stresses of travel, Randolph grew steadily sicker. Although he appeared to recover in mid-January and regain some of his strength, he soon suffered a relapse.

On February 12, 1886, Randolph Caldecott died. The attending physician described the cause of death as "organic disease of the heart." He was buried in Evergreen Cemetery in St. Augustine, Florida.

Bright and colorful, this painting, "All on a Summer's Day," captures the energy from the book The Queen of Hearts.

CHAPTER 7

THE CALDECOTT MEDAL

andolph's work would outlive him. Every year more and more of his books were reprinted. Many of his individual illustrations were sold at galleries and displayed in museums.

But his lasting fame came half a century after his death.

In 1937, a publisher named Frederic C. Melcher had an idea which would guarantee that the Caldecott name and the work he did would endure for generations.

Fifteen years earlier, Melcher had established the Newbery Award to honor the author of the best children's book published each year. It soon became apparent to many people that children's book illustrators were just as deserving of recognition as the authors.

So Melcher proposed an award that, according to the American Library Association (ALA) website, "shall be awarded to the artist of the most distinguished American Picture Book for Children published in the United States during the preceding year. The award shall go to the artist, who must be a citizen or resident of the United States, whether or not he be the author of the text."

There was no doubt about the person after whom the award would be named: Randolph Caldecott.

Melcher later wrote down his reasons for naming the medal after Caldecott, saying, "it supplies us with a name that has pleasant memories—memories connected with the joyousness of picture books as well as with their beauty. Whatever direction new books may take, I think that joyous and gentle approach is one thing we should be gently reminded of."

Melcher proposed his idea at the annual meeting of the American Library Association. It was accepted.

Beginning in 1938, an illustrator has been awarded the Caldecott Medal every year. It is one of the most prestigious prizes in children's literature. Despite his all-too-brief life, Randolph Caldecott's joyous drawings have served as a gentle reminder not just of an approach to art, but to life itself.

Above: The Girl I Left Behind Me. After his death, Randolph Caldecott's works were displayed in galleries and museums. This painting was shown at the Manchester Jubilee in 1887 and then at the Royal Manchester Institution in 1896.

Left: Cover of Babes in the Wood. *The cover of this book indicates that what's inside is not a forest.*

THE CALDECOTT MEDAL

2003: *My Friend Rabbit* by Eric Rohmann (Roaring Brook Press/Milbrook Press)

2002: *The Three Pigs* by David Wiesner (Clarion/Houghton Mifflin)

2001: *So You Want to Be President?* Illustrated by David Small; text by Judith St. George (Philomel Books)

2000: *Joseph Had a Little Overcoat* by Simms Taback (Viking)

1999: *Snowflake Bentley* illustrated by Mary Azarian; text by Jacqueline Briggs Martin (Houghton)

1998: *Rapunzel* by Paul O. Zelinsky (Dutton)

1997: *Golem* by David Wisniewski (Clarion)

1996: *Officer Buckle and Gloria* by Peggy Rathmann (Putnam)

1995: *Smoky Night* illustrated by David Diaz; text by Eve Bunting (Harcourt)

1994: *Grandfather's Journey* by Allen Say; text edited by Walter Lorraine (Houghton)

1993: *Mirette on the High Wire* by Emily Arnold McCully (Putnam)

1992: *Tuesday* by David Wiesner (Clarion Books)

1991: *Black and White* by David Macaulay (Houghton)

1990: *Lon Po Po: A Red-Riding Hood Story from China* by Ed Young (Philomel)

1989: *Song and Dance Man* illustrated by Stephen Gammell; text: Karen Ackerman (Knopf)

1988: *Owl Moon* illustrated by John Schoenherr; text by Jane Yolen (Philomel)

1987: *Hey, Al* illustrated by Richard Egielski; text by Arthur Yorinks (Farrar)

1986: *The Polar Express* by Chris Van Allsburg (Houghton)

1985: *Saint George and the Dragon* illustrated by Trina Schart Hyman; text retold by Margaret Hodges (Little, Brown)

1984: *The Glorious Flight: Across the Channel with Louis Bleriot* by Alice and Martin Provensen (Viking)

1983: *Shadow* illustrated and translated by Marcia Brown; original text in French by Blaise Cendrars (Scribner)

1982: *Jumanji* by Chris Van Allsburg (Houghton)

1981: *Fables* by Arnold Lobel (Harper)

1980: *Ox-Cart Man* illustrated by Barbara Cooney; text by Donald Hall (Viking)

1979: *The Girl Who Loved Wild Horses* by Paul Goble (Bradbury)

1978: *Noah's Ark* by Peter Spier (Doubleday)

1977: *Ashanti to Zulu: African Traditions* illustrated by Leo and Diane Dillon; text by Margaret Musgrove (Dial)

1976: *Why Mosquitoes Buzz in People's Ears* illustrated by Leo & Diane Dillon; text retold by Verna Aardema (Dial)

1975: *Arrow to the Sun* by Gerald McDermott (Viking)

1974: *Duffy and the Devil* illustrated by Margot Zemach; test retold by Harve Zemach (Farrar)

1973: *The Funny Little Woman* illustrated by Blair Lent; text retold by Arlene Mosel (Dutton)

1972: *One Fine Day* illustrated and retold by Nonny Hogrogian (Macmillan)

1971: *A Story A Story* illustrated and retold by Gail E. Haley (Atheneum)

1970: *Sylvester and the Magic Pebble* by William Steig (Windmill Books)

1969: *The Fool of the World and the Flying Ship* illustrated by Uri Shulevitz, text retold by Arthur Ransome (Farrar)

1968: *Drummer Hoff* illustrated by Ed Emberley, text adapted by Barbara Emberley (Prentice-Hall)

1967: *Sam, Bangs & Moonshine* by Evaline Ness (Holt)

1966: *Always Room for One More* illustrated by Nonny Hogrogian, text by Sorche Nic Leodhas, pseudonym [Leclair Alger] (Holt)

1965: *May I Bring a Friend?* illustrated by Beni Montresor, text by Beatrice Schenk de Regniers (Atheneum)

1964: *Where the Wild Things Are* by Maurice Sendak (Harper)

1963: *The Snowy Day* by Ezra Jack Keats (Viking)

1962: *Once a Mouse* illustrated and retold by Marcia Brown (Scribner)

1961: *Baboushka and the Three Kings* illustrated by Nicolas Sidjakov, text by Ruth Robbins (Parnassus)

1960: *Nine Days to Christmas* illustrated by Marie Hall Ets, text by Marie Hall Ets and Aurora Labastida (Viking)

1959: *Chanticleer and the Fox* illustrated by Barbara Cooney, text adapted from Chaucer's *Canterbury Tales* by Barbara Cooney (Crowell)

1958: *Time of Wonder* by Robert McCloskey (Viking)

1957: *A Tree Is Nice* illustrated by Marc Simont, text by Janice Udry (Harper)

1956: *Frog Went A-Courtin'* illustrated by Feodor Rojankovsky, text retold by John Langstaff (Harcourt)

1955: *Cinderella, or the Little Glass Slipper* illustrated by Marcia Brown, text translated from Charles Perrault by Marcia Brown (Scribner)

1954: *Madeline's Rescue* by Ludwig Bemelmans (Viking)

1953: *The Biggest Bear* by Lynd Ward (Houghton)

1952: *Finders Keepers* illustrated by Nicolas, pseudonym [Nicholas Mordvinoff]; text by Will, pseudonym [William Lipkind] (Harcourt)

1951: *The Egg Tree* by Katherine Milhous (Scribner)

1950: *Song of the Swallows* by Leo Politi (Scribner)

1949: *The Big Snow* by Berta and Elmer Hader (Macmillan)

1948: *White Snow, Bright Snow* illustrated by Roger Duvoisin, text by Alvin Tresselt (Lothrop)

1947: *The Little Island* illustrated by Leonard Weisgard, text by Golden MacDonald, pseudonym [Margaret Wise Brown] (Doubleday)

1946: *The Rooster Crows* by Maude and Miska Petersham (Macmillan)

1945: *Prayer for a Child* illustrated by Elizabeth Orton Jones, text by Rachel Field (Macmillan)

1944: *Many Moons* illustrated by Louis Slobodkin, text by James Thurber (Harcourt)

1943: *The Little House* by Virginia Lee Burton (Houghton)

1942: *Make Way for Ducklings* by Robert McCloskey (Viking)

1941: *They Were Strong and Good*, by Robert Lawson (Viking)

1940: *Abraham Lincoln* by Ingri and Edgar Parin d'Aulaire (Doubleday)

1939: *Mei Li* by Thomas Handforth (Doubleday)

1938: *Animals of the Bible, A Picture Book* illustrated by Dorothy P. Lathrop, text selected by Helen Dean Fish (Lippincott)

1846	Born on March 22 in Chester, England
1852	Mother Mary Dinah dies
1850s	Begins attending The Kings School
1861	Drops out of school and begins working as bank clerk in Whitchurch, Shropshire
1861	Sells first illustration to a London newspaper
1867	Begins new job as banker in Manchester and takes classes at Manchester School of Art
1869	Joins Brasenose Club in Manchester
1870	Visits London and shows portfolio to artist Thomas Armstrong
1872	Moves to London, attends the Slade School
1873	First book containing his illustrations is published – *Harz Mountains: A Tour in Toy Country*
1875	Washington Irving's *Old Christmas* is published
1877	Washington Irving's *Bracebridge Hall* is published
1878	First two illustrated children's books, *John Gilpin* and *The House That Jack Built,* are published
1879	Elected member of Manchester Academy of Fine Arts
1880	Marries Marian Brind
1882	Moves to Broomfield, Surrey collaborates with Juliana Horatia Ewing
1883	Illustrates *Aesop's Fables*
1885	Travels to United States
1886	dies in Florida on February 12

1843	Charles Dickens publishes *A Christmas Carol*.
1845	American inventor Peter Cooper patents sugary dessert made of gelatin, which eventually becomes known as Jell-O.
1848	A revolt in France leads to revolutions across Europe.
1850	During California Gold Rush, Levi Strauss begins selling the first jeans.
1854	English poet Alfred Lord Tennyson writes *The Charge of the Light Brigade*.
1861	United States Civil War begins.
1862	President Abraham Lincoln signs the Emancipation Proclamation, freeing slaves as of January 1, 1863.
1865	Civil War ends; President Lincoln is assassinated.
1869	The Union Pacific and Central Pacific Railroads meet in Utah as the first track across the United States is completed.
1876	Mark Twain publishes *The Adventures of Tom Sawyer*; Alexander Graham Bell patents the telephone.
1877	Thomas Edison invents the phonograph.
1880	Edison invents the electric light.
1883	Robert Louis Stevenson publishes *Treasure Island*.
1884	Mark Twain publishes *Huckleberry Finn*.
1888	George Eastman invents Kodak box camera.

FURTHER RECOMMENDED READING

FOR YOUNG ADULTS

Aesop's Fables, compiled by Russell Ash and Bernard Higton. San Francisco: Chronicle Books, 1990.

Billington, Elizabeth. *The Randolph Caldecott Treasury*. New York: Frederick Warne Publishing, 1978.

Caldecott, Randolph. *Yours Pictorially: Illustrated Letters of Randolph Caldecott*. London: Frederick Warne Publishing, 1976.

WORKS CONSULTED

Davis, Mary Gould. *Randolph Caldecott: An Appreciation*. New York: J.B. Lippincott and Company, 1946.

Engen, Rodney K. *Randolph Caldecott: Lord of the Nursery*. London: Oresko Books, 1976.

Smith, Irene. *A History of the Newbery and Caldecott Medals*. New York: Viking Press, 1957.

Welsh, Charles. *A Bookseller of the Last Century*. Clifton, NJ: Augustus M. Kelley, 1972.

ON THE WEB

http://.ala.org/alsc/caldecott

http://www.rcsamerica.com

http://www.randolphcaldecott.org.uk

commission (cum-MISH -on) - work given to an artist by a wealthy patron

engraver (en-GRAY-ver) - person whose job is to carve the impressions from an artist's drawings, usually on a block of wood

illustrator (Ill-us-tray-tor) - artist who draws pictures for books

mentor (MEN-tore) - person who guides and directs someone else

minutes - notes or recordings from a meeting

patron (PAY-trun) - supporter of an artist

refectory (ree-FECK-tor-ee) - room in church or religious institution where meals are served

rheumatic (roo-MAT-ick) fever - severe contagious disease which mainly affects children; symptoms include high fever and swollen joints and it often results in permenant heart damage

sui generis (SOO-ee JEN-ur-is) - something unique